T0198636

EMERGENCY
KIT

Survival Guide to Abundance

Dr. Robin Wallace

BALBOA.
PRESS

A DIVISION OF HAY HOUSE

Balboa Press books may be ordered through booksellers or by contacting:

Balboa Press
A Division of Hay House
1663 Liberty Drive
Bloomington, IN 47403
www.balboapress.com
1 (877) 407-4847

Because of the dynamic nature of the Internet, any web addresses or links contained in this book may have changed since publication and may no longer be valid. The views expressed in this work are solely those of the author and do not necessarily reflect the views of the publisher, and the publisher hereby disclaims any responsibility for them.

The author of this book does not dispense medical advice or prescribe the use of any technique as a form of treatment for physical, emotional, or medical problems without the advice of a physician, either directly or indirectly. The intent of the author is only to offer information of a general nature to help you in your quest for emotional and spiritual well-being. In the event you use any of the information in this book for yourself, which is your constitutional right, the author and the publisher assume no responsibility for your actions.

Any people depicted in stock imagery provided by Thinkstock are models, and such images are being used for illustrative purposes only. Certain stock imagery © Thinkstock.

Print information available on the last page.

ISBN: 978-1-5043-3496-9 (sc)
ISBN: 978-1-5043-3497-6 (e)

Library of Congress Control Number: 2015909777

Balboa Press rev. date: 8/27/2015

CONTENTS

INTRODUCTION

Emergency Kit is for people who are having crises with the conflicting thoughts, beliefs, and feelings of their conscious selves versus their subconscious. These crises can be triggered by emergencies, by which I mean unexpected and unwanted occurrences in life: for example, the sudden loss of a loved one, a relationship, or a job. Or you may experience a disappointment of some kind: a financial setback, a promotion that didn't come through, weight gain, or a health challenge; the list can go on and on.

Feelings of fear, pain, doubt, resentment, anger, and lack can come over you so quickly that you don't even realize why you're feeling so bad—and these feelings can linger long after an event has passed. Days, weeks, months, and sometimes years go by, and still you continue to act and feel as if the emergency were happening today—and guess what? You are completely unaware of it; you don't have a clue what's lurking in the subconscious.

After a string of past emergencies that still affect you today, you may be constantly wondering, "Why haven't any of my dreams come true? Why am I always stuck on the same page of my life?" You may even be discouraged by the tons of self-help books, tapes, seminars, and affirmations that were supposed to work but haven't. This can happen to anyone. Even people familiar with *The Secret* and the law of attraction can lose sight of their intentions.

Sometimes your mind quickly runs toward negativity. Get that speeding train off its current track of doubt, fear, lack, and the constant focus on what you don't want. Get back on the track of your positive intentions, and focus only on what you *do* want.

THE SELF: CONSCIOUS OF THE SUBCONSCIOUS

To better help you through this ongoing state of emergency in your mind, I have included in the first chapter an example of what a conversation between the conscious self and the subconscious might sound like. In this dialogue, the self—usually unconscious and unaware of the deep-rooted emotions and negative conditions of the subconscious—begins to get a sense of the influence that the subconscious has on it. The subconscious accepts and holds on to the constantly affirmed beliefs, feelings, and emotions of the self. This is the missing piece in many self-help books I have read. That is—if the self is unaware of the subconscious condition, whether positive or negative, the reaction of the subconscious is what creates your surroundings and results.

Who is really speaking? Is it the old, deeply ingrained patterns of the subconscious, which, in a state of emergency, are the unwanted feelings and thoughts that continue to percolate your conscious mind? The old patterns of negative thinking you have never let go of? Or is it the self, speaking from a place of new, positive awakening?

In this state of emergency, the self needs to be conscious as to what it really believes, to be aware of what's going on in the subconscious. If your self is speaking positively, but you really don't believe it, then something contrary to that positive, abundant affirmation is still held tightly in the subconscious—a contradictory condition or pattern that produces the same negative results.

The good news is that when the self is conscious of its feelings and where those emotions come from, an emergency can be but a moment in your life instead of morphing into negative patterns that get entrenched in the subconscious. As you move forward with a positive affirmation as to what you *do* want, the subconscious begins to accept the affirmations and visualizations of the new, positive self. The result can, therefore, only be positive.

If the dialogue in chapter 1 sounds or feels familiar, please take a few minutes to complete the exercises presented in the kit in chapter 3. Not only will these tools help you move out of emergency mode, but they will also place your self and subconscious into a life only you and God can create—a life of what you *do* want!

A DIALOGUE

Below is an example of a conversation between the self and the subconscious, if the subconscious could speak its hidden thoughts, beliefs, and feelings to the self while in emergency mode.

SELF,
standing naked in front of a mirror
Yes, I can!
Yes, I can!
Yes, I can!

SUBCONSCIOUS
Oh yeah, those were the days, admiring
yourself in front of the mirror.
We are not as confident since the emergency.

SELF

Yes, I can!

I love and approve of myself.

All is well in my world. I am in a loving space.

SUBCONSCIOUS

I do not love and approve of myself—screw the world!

SELF

I am now a size four and looking good.

SUBCONSCIOUS

Who are you trying to kid? You

are a large size four*teen.*

SELF

I am now accepting a wonderful new

high-paying job and ... and ...

SUBCONSCIOUS

How much?

SELF

Right ... okay, I am a money magnet.

I now accept a wonderful new job worth millions.

SUBCONSCIOUS

Hmmm, really?

How much are you really worth?

Millions feels a little high; come down a bit.

And say it with more feeling.

SELF

I am a thousandaire!

SUBCONSCIOUS

How are you going to create that kind of wealth?

SELF

I'm not supposed to worry about the
how, just the *what.* Duh.

SUBCONSCIOUS

Okay, smarty pants, what do you want?

SELF

I don't know.

SUBCONSCIOUS

Therein lies the problem. If you don't know, I will be
happy to continue our negative habits. A *whole cake*
sounds good about now—we are in an *emergency!*

SELF

I stare down the tunnel of my eyes
into my soul. I believe!

SUBCONSCIOUS

Nice try! *I didn't feel that at all!*
You're not even looking into your eyes.

SELF

Yes, I can? Yes, I can. Yes, I *can!*

SUBCONSCIOUS

Guess what? No, you can't! Just look at you! The nerve
of you to say that, standing there naked. Put your clothes
back on. What were you thinking? Eating your feelings
has made you obese, and your job sucks! You're resentful
because you lost your spirit. *Yes, I can?* Self, please!

SELF/SUBCONSCIOUS

No, I can't.

SUBCONSCIOUS

No, you cannot settle for mediocrity.
Mediocrity is easier—a box of donuts for breakfast.
Sound familiar?

SELF

I can start over on Monday. Give your Self a break.

SUBCONSCIOUS

That's right. We've been thinking this way for years.
Put off changing till tomorrow.

SELF/SUBCONSCIOUS

Thank God we settled that! That was exhausting.

SUBCONSCIOUS

Putting things off feels good, Self ... as
comforting as a gigantic, crunchy carbo-cookie
or an octuple bacon cheeseburger.

SELF

I have nothing to wear. Nothing fits. I'm so fat.
How can anybody love this?
I hate my life. I shoulda, coulda, woulda ...

SUBCONSCIOUS

Oh, please don't run to the bathroom mirror again!

SELF

I love myself! I mean it! I love and approve of myself!
Yes, I can. God is my Source. What do I want?

SUBCONSCIOUS

Yeah! Don't forget to say ...

SELF

Live in the *now!* I live in the now, loving and approving of myself in a kick-ass loving relationship. My partner loves what I love—no couch-potato living for us—and oh yeah, is also great in bed and someone I can trust. I am a size-two muscular millionaire with an adorable dog.

SUBCONSCIOUS

Don't forget anything, because it won't come true if you miss one itty-bitty thing.

SELF

I love myself? Then why do I feel so miserable?

SUBCONSCIOUS

Go ahead; it's okay. Pick up the phone.

SELF/SUBCONSCIOUS

Hi, it's Self. I'm not coming in to work today. I'm sick.

SUBCONSCIOUS

Now, Self, go ahead and cry. You deserve it.

SELF

Oh, it feels so good.

SELF/SUBCONSCIOUS

I will now tightly hug the pillow and snuggle
up to my dog, who is very concerned.

SUBCONSCIOUS

Look how worried my dog is. I love you,
my sweet pet. I will be okay.
Self is just loathing herself.

SELF

Changing into my pa-jay-jays. I am sick today!

SUBCONSCIOUS

Check.

SELF

Closing the blinds.

SUBCONSCIOUS

Check.

SELF

Concerned pet to snuggle with, bonbons,
chips, ringer is off, remote control, tissues …

SUBCONSCIOUS

Check, check, check, check, check, check.

(Several hours go by—or perhaps days, months, years.)

SELF

I am so happy, I am so thankful, I am so
grateful—now that I am in my bed.
No worries, responsibilities, or inner-healing
workshops. Tomorrow is another day.

SELF/SUBCONSCIOUS

I'm not good enough. I'm a loser. I'm never going to
fulfill my dreams. Other people get all the breaks. I look
at food and gain weight. I just don't have the energy to
make it happen. What if I'm not saying the right things
to God? What if I forget something? I'm not worthy
of having a healthy relationship, financial freedom, and
perfect health. I don't know what I want. I can't do this.
I can't, I can't, I can't, I won't, I won't, I won't, I'm not,
I'm not, I'm not.

SUBCONSCIOUS

Well, give yourself a break and don't worry about it.
You can start all over again tomorrow or Monday.

SELF

Ahh, so miserable. Sweet dreams!

GOD

Get your butt up!

SELF

What?

SUBCONSCIOUS

Uh-oh! Self, wake up!

SELF

What time is it? Can't seem to get back to sleep.

SUBCONSCIOUS

We're in trouble now.

SELF/SUBCONSCIOUS

I should have gone to work today.

SELF

I don't want to think about that.

SUBCONSCIOUS/SELF

Look at this great opportunity to just say
screw it. This is my time to sulk.

SELF/SUBCONSCIOUS

Maybe I can go in to work in the afternoon.

SELF

What am I doing?

GOD

Get up!

HIGHER POWER

You can do it!

SELF

God, is that you?

SUBCONSCIOUS

Yup, that's God, your Higher Power, or whatever label you're comfortable with.

SELF

God, help me, please.

SUBCONSCIOUS

Louder!

SELF

Help me!

HIGHER POWER

Get up!

SELF

It hurts, it's hard, I can't, and I don't want to get up.

GOD

This old, negative condition will not get
better unless you change your actions.

SELF

Okay. It is time to do the work.

HIGHER POWER

Let's start with the basics.

SELF

Okay.

SUBCONSCIOUS

Okay.

HIGHER POWER

Do you love yourself?
If you say yes and mean it, we can move on.

SELF

Yes.

SUBCONSCIOUS

Wait a minute. I'm not sure.

SELF

Going to the mirror.

GOD/HIGHER POWER

Yes! Really know and believe that you love
yourself, that you can receive! Feel it!

SELF/SUBCONSCIOUS

I unconditionally, absolutely love myself, and I am ready
to live up to my highest potential, so thank you, God.

SELF

I'm tired of being miserable.

SUBCONSCIOUS

I'm exhausted.

GOD/HIGHER POWER

Lean on me. I am never tired and am
always ready to give you your gifts.
Are you ready?

SELF/SUBCONSCIOUS

Yes! I am ready.

CHAPTER 2

WHAT DO YOU WANT?

This dialogue is one I have had with myself. During a crisis, your subconscious often remains in a negative condition even though your self is making all the effort in the world to be positive. When the self is conscious of its thoughts, beliefs, and emotions, eventually they will be accepted by the subconscious as truth or law. Because of this, it is essential that you discipline yourself to consciously affirm, believe, and express what you *do* want out of life. If it is joy, think joyful thoughts.

Be aware that like attracts like. If your thoughts and beliefs are constantly negative, especially the subtle thoughts and beliefs ingrained in the subconscious, you will attract negative conditions. Whether you believe this or not, the law of attraction is true and has been proven in every generation by those who consciously apply it. The only way to shift negative patterns is to get the self and its subconscious in tune with each other. As you move forward in your practice, condition your mind to think positive thoughts. Eventually the subconscious will adopt your powerful, positive thoughts and beliefs, and it will be on the same frequency as your conscious self. Both will then work together for your highest good.

Perhaps you go around confidently applying the law of attraction for a better, more positive, and abundant life. But during a crisis—a job loss, a failing relationship, financial problems, poor health, or even simple frustrations—it often happens that the *wants* you have been obsessing over are no longer being easily met. This can create a crisis in itself, putting you in a state of emergency. The self then struggles to speak the law of attraction. Tools you have used from *The Secret* now seem dull, and the vision of attracting wealth in all areas of your life is blurred.

As soon as the self loses interest in speaking what you *do* want, stop! The subconscious has now been overpowered by the strong feelings and beliefs stemming from the self's struggle and its undue focus on the emergency—a clear message to your subconscious of what you *don't* want. Remember—like attracts like, whether positive or negative. You will unfailingly receive more of what the subconscious believes to be true. The thoughts and beliefs of the subconscious determine your results.

In an emergency, you are struggling to get back on track, to be the master of your mind and thoughts. If you are not clear on what to do at that moment, you can become confused and overpowered by an illusion that you are heading in the right direction when you are actually moving in the wrong direction. Firefighters speak of this experience when they are battling a fire: the fire and smoke, as well as the emergency itself, can stir up emotions of fear and confusion. Even experienced firefighters can get lost in the blaze, losing their sense of direction and making bad decisions.

In a state of emergency, resentment toward your life can arise, and strong emotions about what you don't want may create undesirable results. The more overpowering the fear that you won't escape the emergency, the greater the likelihood that you'll get lost in the smoke. You know you've made the wrong decision when you abandon thinking about what you *do* want for what you *don't* want.

This condition of emergency can cause you to send out negative frequencies that will attract more unwanted, negative thoughts, creating a vicious cycle. Recognize this pattern of dialogue. Use this unwanted condition as a stimulus to shift into positive thoughts. Attract what you want into your life by asking yourself what you want. You can intentionally change your thoughts and frequency and shift out of emergency mode. Then, through the law of attraction, what comes into your life will shift toward the positive.

SHIFTING THE CONDITION

Manifest all the good you want in your life. Lift yourself out of the feelings of a state of emergency by completing the "What Do You Want?" portion of the kit in Chapter 3. The key to this section is to make sure you are ready to claim your life. Feel good about what you are going to accomplish. Choose a quiet room without distractions, turn on your favorite music if you wish, and meditate on what you want in each area of your life. Then write down each goal in the present tense; believe and visualize yourself having it *right now.*

Feel good about what you are declaring, and when you read it back to yourself, make sure it feels good—believe you have it already. Feel love, gratitude, and confidence behind every thought and word you write down. Then declare that you want it now!

Dare to believe that you can have everything you want, believe that you deserve it, and have faith that it is your birthright to receive it. If it came from you, then it came from God. The Universe wants you to be your very best and receive everything you want. Do not worry about the *how, when,* and *where.* The Universe, or God, will take care of that. All you have to do is feel wonderful about this process, feel happy about *what* you have written, and trust that you will attract what you want.

Make sure you speak your words in the present tense as if you already have what you want. You must feel good about what you want, and you will receive it. Know it; feel it. Know you deserve it. Claim your life experience—it is that simple. Speak it into action, and it is yours. Think big! It should inspire you. Repeat each declaration until you feel you have it *now.* Be grateful for what you are manifesting into your life. The more you practice it, the more effortless it will be. Enjoy yourself, have fun, love the process, and be ready to receive—now!

In the next chapter, please fill out your *wants* in each category. Be clear and specific. These are the *wants,* wrapped in love and gratitude, that will show up in your life.

Stay positive and focused. Take advantage of your opportunity to heal old ways of thinking such as negativity and lack, and successfully and positively move into a lifestyle of love, abundance, and wealth in all areas of your life.

Declare what you want to attract into your life. This is your chance; you are in the moment of your greatness.

CHAPTER 3

THE KIT

Let's start with listing under each category three things you would like to manifest in your life—what you *do* want. As you are doing this, feel each goal, visualize it, and declare you want it *now!* Be grateful and love yourself. Then believe you have already received it—your divine birthright.

To get started, please go to next page.

SELF

What do you want personally?

1.

2.

3.

Self/Subconscious

When do you want it?

Now!

SELF

What do you want personally?

1.

2.

3.

Self/Subconscious

When do you want it?

Now!

SELF

What do you want personally?

1.

2.

3.

Self/Subconscious

When do you want it?

Now!

CREATE YOUR OWN VISION BOARD HERE

SELF

What do you want in a relationship?

1.

2.

3.

Self-Subconscious

When do you want it?

Now!

SELF

What do you want in a relationship?

1.

2.

3.

Self-Subconscious

When do you want it?

Now!

SELF

What do you want in a relationship?

1.

2.

3.

Self-Subconscious

When do you want it?

Now!

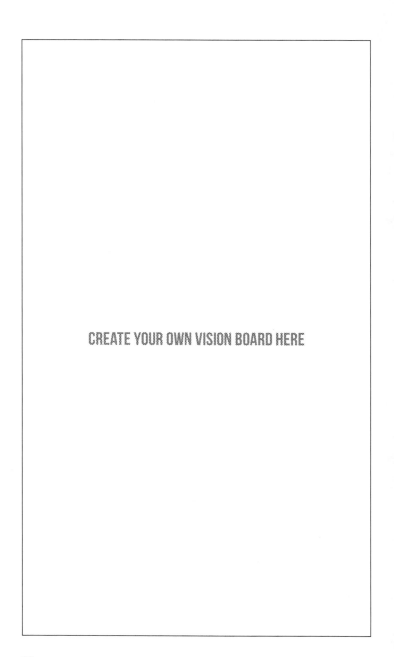

CREATE YOUR OWN VISION BOARD HERE

SELF

What do you want for your health/body?

1.

2.

3.

Self-Subconscious

When do you want it?

Now!

SELF

What do you want for your health/body?

1.

2.

3.

Self-Subconscious

When do you want it?

Now!

SELF

What do you want for your health/body?

1.

2.

3.

Self-Subconscious

When do you want it?

Now!

CREATE YOUR OWN VISION BOARD HERE

SELF

What do you want for your career or education?

1.

2.

3.

Self-Subconscious

When do you want it?

Now!

SELF

What do you want for your career or education?

1.

2.

3.

Self-Subconscious

When do you want it?

Now!

SELF

What do you want for your career or education?

1.

2.

3.

Self-Subconscious

When do you want it?

Now!

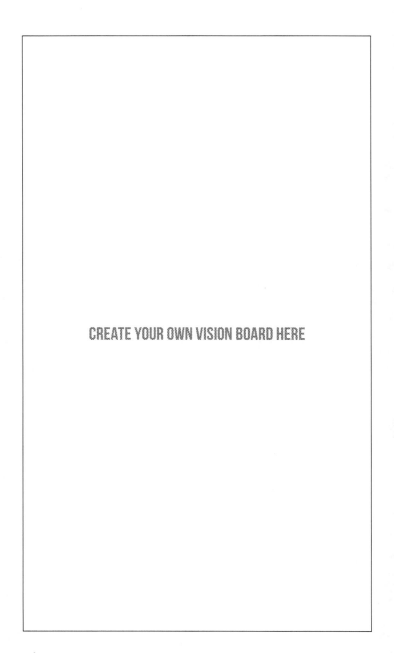

CREATE YOUR OWN VISION BOARD HERE

SELF

What do you want in your recreation or hobbies?

1.

2.

3.

Self-Subconscious

When do you want it?

Now!

SELF

What do you want in your recreation or hobbies?

1.

2.

3.

Self-Subconscious

When do you want it?

Now!

SELF

What do you want in your recreation or hobbies?

1.

2.

3.

Self-Subconscious

When do you want it?

Now!

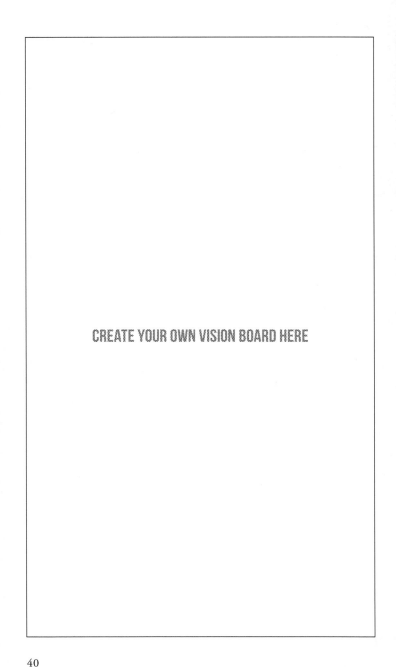

CREATE YOUR OWN VISION BOARD HERE

SELF

What do you want for your finances?

1.

2.

3.

Self-Subconscious

When do you want it?

Now!

SELF

What do you want for your finances?

1.

2.

3.

Self-Subconscious

When do you want it?

Now!

SELF

What do you want for your finances?

1.

2.

3.

Self-Subconscious

When do you want it?

Now!

CREATE YOUR OWN VISION BOARD HERE

SELF

What do you want to accomplish through
your charitable contributions?

1.

2.

3.

Self-Subconscious

When do you want it?

Now!

SELF

What do you want to accomplish through
your charitable contributions?

1.

2.

3.

Self-Subconscious

When do you want it?

Now!

SELF

What do you want to accomplish through
your charitable contributions?

1.

2.

3.

Self-Subconscious

When do you want it?

Now!

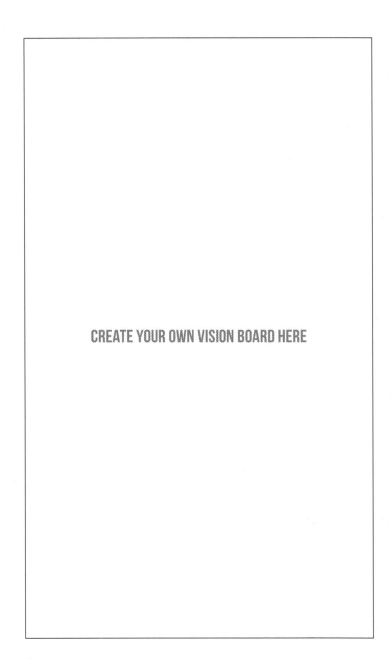

CREATE YOUR OWN VISION BOARD HERE

SELF

What do you want spiritually?

1.

2.

3.

Self-Subconscious

When do you want it?

Now!

SELF

What do you want spiritually?

1.

2.

3.

Self-Subconscious

When do you want it?

Now!

SELF

What do you want spiritually?

1.

2.

3.

Self-Subconscious

When do you want it?

Now!

CREATE YOUR OWN VISION BOARD HERE

CHAPTER 4

THE WAKE-UP

SELF/SUBCONSCIOUS

Hey, we can do this!

SELF

It feels good to take responsibility for my life.

SUBCONSCIOUS

Looking in the mirror, I see no shame,
discomfort, regret, animosity, pain, resentment,
doubt, fear, lack, or negativity.

SELF

Yes, I love myself. I'm moving forward in
a loving, prosperous, abundant way.

SUBCONSCIOUS

We are on the same page.

SELF

Yes! Do the work. Focus on what I *do* want. That is what will be true to the Universe/ God/Higher Power and my subconscious.

SELF/SUBCONSCIOUS

What do you want? Prosperity!
When do you want it? Now!

SELF/SUBCONSCIOUS

Wow! That feels great!

SUBCONSCIOUS

I want to thank you.

SELF

For what?

SELF/SUBCONSCIOUS

For believing in us. Whenever you have a moment, I will make sure you go into your tools of knowing. I've got your back.

GOD

I've got your back!

HIGHER POWER

I've got your back!

GOD/HIGHER POWER

As long as you believe, I've got your back.

SELF

I believe! Thank you so much! Amen!

CHAPTER 5

YOU DID IT!

This emergency kit is a quick reminder to get you back on track, back to what you *do* want. Now that you're out of crisis mode, I encourage you to cut out the "What Do You Want?" sections of this kit—and practice. Every day be happy and grateful that you are receiving everything you have thoughtfully written down—-and more. You are now in control of your destiny.

Wishing you many blessings.

ABOUT THE AUTHOR

Dr. Robin Wallace received a bachelor's degree in psychology with a minor in anthropology from Connecticut College, and she earned a doctorate of oriental medicine from the International Institute of Chinese Medicine in Santa Fe, New Mexico, followed by an internship at the China–Japan Friendship Hospital in Beijing, China. Dr. Wallace's exposure to body-mind medicine and Science of Mind practices influenced the inspiration she offers in *The Emergency Kit*. Dr. Wallace implements a metaphysical acupuncture practice and lifestyle—"What you think is what you attract."—that has helped her patients move through their current symptoms into relief by envisioning their ideal lives.

Printed in the United States
By Bookmasters